Trumpets

MUSICAL INSTRUMENTS

Cynthia Amoroso,
Robert B. Noyed,
and John Willis

LET'S READ
AV2 BY WEIGL
ADDED VALUE · AUDIO VISUAL

www.av2books.com

LET'S READ

AV²
BY WEIGL™

ADDED VALUE • AUDIO VISUAL

Go to **www.av2books.com**, and enter this book's unique code.

BOOK CODE

C 5 4 3 4 9 6

AV² by Weigl brings you media enhanced books that support active learning.

AV² provides enriched content that supplements and complements this book. Weigl's AV² book strive to create inspired learning and engage young minds in a total learning experience.

Your AV² Media Enhanced books come alive with...

Audio
Listen to sections of the book read aloud.

Key Words
Study vocabulary, and complete a matching word activity.

Video
Watch informative video clips.

Quizzes
Test your knowledge.

Embedded Weblinks
Gain additional information for research.

Slide Show
View images and captions, and prepare a presentation.

Try This!
Complete activities and hands-on experiments.

... and much, much more!

Published by AV² by Weigl
350 5th Avenue, 59th Floor   New York, NY   10118
Website: www.av2books.com

Library of Congress Control Number: 2017936397

ISBN 978-1-4896-6013-8 (hardcover)
ISBN 978-1-4896-6014-5 (softcover)
ISBN 978-1-4896-6015-2 (multi-user eBook)

Printed in the United States of America in Brainerd, Minnesota
1 2 3 4 5 6 7 8 9 0   21 20 19 18 17

042017
310117

Project Coordinator: John Willis   Designer: Nick Newton

Weigl acknowledges Getty Images, Alamy, iStock, and Shutterstock as the primary image suppliers for this title.

MUSICAL INSTRUMENTS

Trumpets

In this book, you will learn about

trumpets

what they are

how you play them

and much more!

4

Watch three fingers move quickly up and down. See the light shining off the horn. Hear the sound. Toot, toot, toot. He is playing the trumpet.

5

A trumpet is a wind instrument made of metal tubing. The metal is curved in an oval shape.

If a trumpet was not curved, it would be more than 6 feet (1.8 meters) long.

8

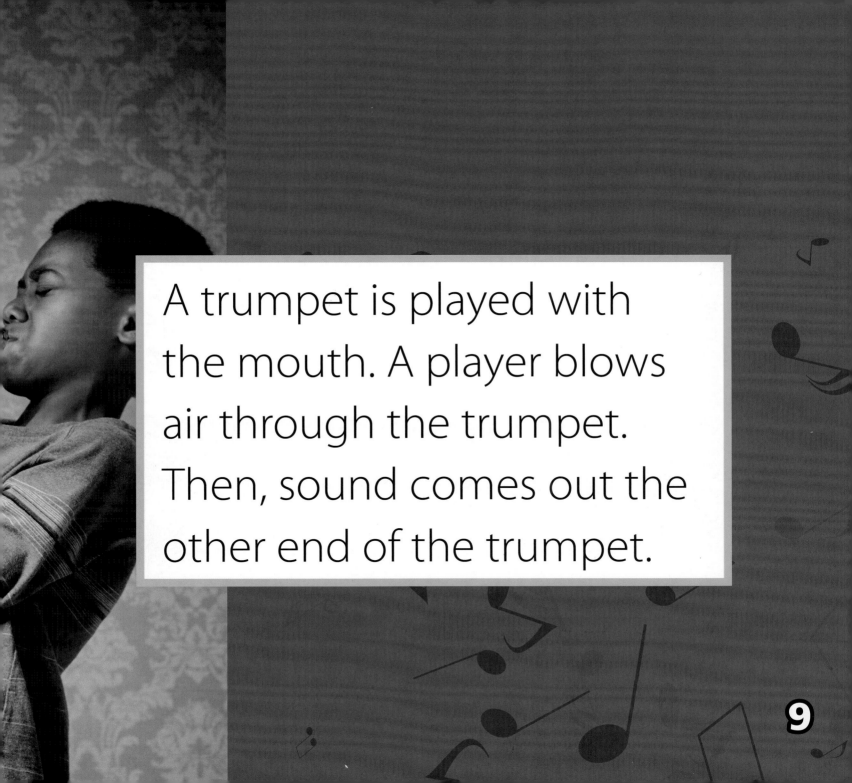

A trumpet is played with the mouth. A player blows air through the trumpet. Then, sound comes out the other end of the trumpet.

The end of the trumpet has a big opening. The metal flares out. This part is called the bell because it has a bell shape.

The smallest kind of trumpet is called a piccolo trumpet.

There are three keys on the trumpet. These keys are called valves. A player makes different sounds by pushing the valves.

13

A player makes sounds by changing the shape of his mouth, too. The lips vibrate while playing the trumpet.

15

The trumpet is an old instrument. People in China played a kind of trumpet thousands of years ago. Now trumpets are played all over the world.

The first metal trumpets were created more than 3,000 years ago.

17

Trumpets are important to many people. Long ago, people used them to make announcements. Today, trumpets are usually played to make music.

Trumpets are important for many kinds of music. Many trumpet players are famous for jazz music. Children play trumpets in school bands.

See what you have learned about trumpets.

Which of these pictures does not show a trumpet?

KEY WORDS

Research has shown that as much as 65 percent of all written material published in English is made up of 300 words. These 300 words cannot be taught using pictures or learned by sounding them out. They must be recognized by sight. This book contains 70 common sight words to help young readers improve their reading fluency and comprehension. This book also teaches young readers several important content words, such as proper nouns. These words are paired with pictures to aid in learning and improve understanding.

Page	Sight Words First Appearance
5	and, down, he, hear, is, light, move, off, see, sound, the, three, up, watch
6	a, an, be, feet, if, in, it, long, made, more, not, of, than, was, would
9	air, comes, end, other, out, then, through, with
10	because, big, has, kind, part, this
12	are, by, different, makes, on, there, these
14	his, too, while
16	all, first, now, old, over, people, were, years
19	important, many, them, to, used
20	children, for, play, school

Page	Content Words First Appearance
5	fingers, horn, trumpet
6	instrument, metal, shape, tubing
9	mouth
10	bell, opening, piccolo trumpet
12	keys, valves
14	lips
16	China
19	announcements, music
20	bands, jazz